Growing up with Grammar 2

First published in Australia in 2003 by New Frontier Publishing
Reprinted in 2005, 2009, 2011
ABN 25 192 683 466
Suite 3, Level 2, 18 Aquatic Drive, Frenchs Forest, NSW 2086 Australia
www.newfrontier.com.au

Cover Illustrations: Marion Kim,   Internal Illustrations: Laura Gulbin

Designed by Ronald Proft

Edited by Kristina Proft

National Library of Australia
Cataloguing-in-Publication data:
Winch, Gordon, 1930-.
Growing Up with Grammar. Book 2

1. English language – Grammar – Juvenile literature.
2. English language – Usage – Juvenile literature.
3. English language – Writing – Juvenile literature.

428

ISBN 0 9750896 76

Acknowledgments
The author would like to thank Lesley Ljungdahl and Paul March,
who acted as academic consultants to this series.

The author would also like to thank the principals and staff of the schools
throughout Australia who assisted in the research leading to the publication of
the Growing up with Grammar series and the Primary Grammar Dictionary.

Special thanks are offered to the following schools:
Beecroft Public School, North Rocks Public School, Northmead Public School,
Pymble Ladies' College, Ravenswood School for Girls, St Gerard's Primary School,
Sydney Grammar Preparatory School and The Hills Grammar School.

Printed by Everbest Printing Co., China

Growing up with Grammar 2

Gordon Winch

Contents

Grammar Units

To the Student

Growing up with Grammar is a book just for you.

There are many interesting things to do.

Grammar

Grammar can be really fun,

You'll find out in this book.

So don't waste time,

Just start right now,

And go and have a *look!*

Have fun!

Gordon Winch

To the Teacher

What the book is

Growing up with Grammar, Book 2 is the second book of four in the *Growing up with Grammar* series that covers the requirements of the primary grammar syllabus in grammar, punctuation and usage with special focus on outcomes and indicators. Book 2 is set at the level of Stage I of the NSW *Syllabus English K-6,* but can be used beyond this.

Why it was written

The series has been written and published following serious research into need and demand in Australian primary schools.

The author

The author is Dr Gordon Winch, a well-known writer and authority in the field of educational texts in English.

What the book contains

Book 2 contains 28 units that teach concepts of grammar, punctuation and usage in the context of a section of text, across a range of Key Learning Areas. Each unit covers a double-page spread and provides clear definitions of grammatical points followed by interesting and varied exercises. "More Action" segments provide follow-on work at the end of each unit and a brief description of the text type is provided at the bottom of each double-page spread.

How the grammar is sequenced

The grammar is taught in Levels, following the sequence Word Level; Phrase and Group Level; Clause and Sentence Level; and Text Level. Correct Word Usage, Punctuation and Figurative Language follow the grammar segments.

Assessment and monitoring

Revision and testing pages are provided at various places in the book to assess the learned material, and outcomes and indicators checklists are also provided at the end of the book. An answer section facilitates individual use of the text and is a resource for the teacher.

How to use the book

The book can be used in a variety of ways: as a text book for each student at a particular level, as a resource for teachers and students who are following a loose-leaf portfolio approach and as a valuable homework grammar text. Its simple structure will allow the teacher to fit the book into his or her program with ease.

It is important to note that the text and others in the series can be used in a number of grades depending on the learning requirements of different schools, classes and students. It is specially designed for flexible use.

For instance, two different books in the series may be used in some classrooms, or one particular book may be used over two years. The material is carefully graded, developmental and covers the primary school syllabus fully.

Primary Grammar Dictionary

The *Growing up with Grammar* series is complementary to the *Primary Grammar Dictionary*. This Dictionary provides easy and immediate reference to all the grammar, punctuation and usage in the *Growing Up with Grammar* series, plus definitions of many other terms and concepts that are found in traditional and functional grammars. It is an essential resource for every student and every teacher. The Dictionary covers the grammar, punctuation and correct word usage requirements of the primary school, from kindergarten/prep. to Year 6.

Overview

The Book at a Glance

28 double-page units of grammar, punctuation and usage

- Covering syllabus content outcomes and indicators at Stage 1.
- In context of literary and factual text types over Key Learning Areas
- At word, phrase and group, clause and sentence, and text levels
- With grammar definitions, text excerpts, varied exercises and "More Action" activities.

4 double-page revision units with "Take A Test" focus

Answer section to all questions

Outcomes and indicators checklists for assessment

Text type description at foot of unit pages

Outcomes	Talking and Listening	TS1.1, TS1.2, TS1.3, TS1.4	(See p. 74)
	Reading	RS1.5, RS1.6, RS1.7, RS1.8	
	Writing	WS1.9, WS1.10, WS1.13, WS1.14	

Indicators (See p. 75)

Key Learning Areas

- Creative Arts K–6
- English K–6
- Human Society and Its Environment K–6
- Personal Development Health and Physical Education K–6
- Science and Technology K–6

Text Type:

FACTUAL RECOUNT

COMMON NOUNS

Nouns are the names of things, like *beach* or *boats*. These common things are called **common nouns**.

At the <u>Beach</u>

We went to the <u>beach</u> in the bus. We saw boys and girls on the sand, with their parents and friends. There were boats and surfers in the sea. I played on the rocks and jumped into the waves. Later we went to the shop and bought an apple and a drink.

1. Draw a line under all the common nouns in the recount. The first two are done for you

2. **a.** Finish the common nouns in the beach picture. Pick from the box.

b. Colour in the beach picture.

boat	surfer	boy	waves
bird	girl	umbrella	dog

b _____

b _____

s _____

w _____

b _____

d _____

u _____

g _____

3. Finish the common nouns. These nouns are other things you saw on the beach. Pick from the box.

bucket   towel   fish   sandcastle   spade

t _____   b _____   f _____

s _____   s _____

4. Colour in the boxes that contain common nouns. They are things you could touch.

water	on	see	flag
sandwich	hat	shout	swim
sat	my	bus	seaweed
dog	big	pool	go

MORE ACTION

- In your own book of folder, write a recount of a holiday, a bush walk, a party or a trip to town. Underline the common nouns.
- Draw your own beach scene. Write nouns to name some of the things you have drawn.

A factual recount tells us about something that happened in the past. The events are described in order, one after another. You will find factual recounts in books about the past, on television, in films and in much of the writing you do yourself.

11

PROPER NOUNS

Proper nouns are the names of people, places and special things, such as *Jack, Australia* or *Monday*. They always start with capital letters.

My Friends

1. Finish this poem with proper nouns. Pick from the box to make the poem rhyme.

Sally	Mick	Jess

Nick and Rick

and Sue and _____.

Dave and Jen and Ali.

Tess and Bess

and Ying and _____ ,

Jack and Josh and _____.

2. Write the names of three of your best friends.

_____   _____   _____

3. In your own book or folder:

  a. Draw your face and write your full name underneath.

  b. Draw your teacher's face and write your teacher's name underneath.

4. Write the names of the following things.

    a. the town or city where you live _____.

    b. the name of your State _____.

    c. the name of your best friend _____.

    d. the month of your birthday _____.

    e. your favourite day of the week _____.

5. Draw a circle around all the proper nouns in these playground rhymes.
Remember that some proper nouns can be more than one word,
like Sydney Harbour Bridge or Maria Jones.

Algy saw the bear.
The bear saw Algy.
The bear was bulgy.
The bulge was Algy.

Sweet little Emily Rose
Sat on a chair to pose,
But young brother Jack
On that chair put a tack –
And sweet little Emily…rose.

Mary had a wristlet watch
She swallowed it one day,
And now she's taking
Beecham's Pills
To pass the time away.

Mrs P
Mrs A
Mrs RRA
Mrs M
Mrs A
Mrs TTA
PARRAMATTA!

MORE ACTION

• In your own books, write a poem using the first names of students
in your class. It does not have to rhyme.

Text Type:

LITERARY DESCRIPTION

DESCRIPTIVE ADJECTIVES

Adjectives are describing words. They tell you more about nouns. *Grey* is an adjective, as in *grey* legs. Grey describes the noun *legs*. It tells you more about them.

Samantha Seagull's Sandals

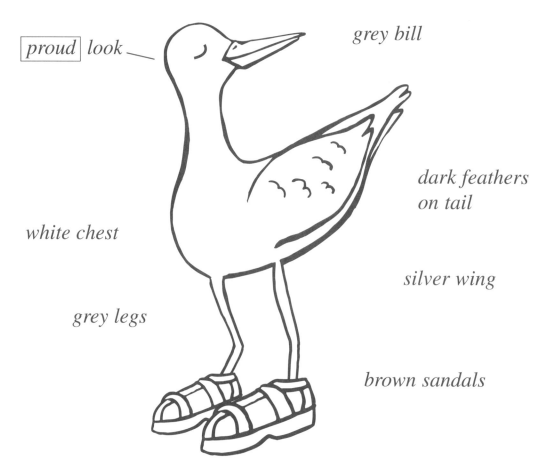

proud look

grey bill

dark feathers on tail

white chest

silver wing

grey legs

brown sandals

1.
a. Draw boxes around the adjectives in these labels. *Proud* is the first one.

b. Draw lines to the correct parts of Samantha. The first one is done for you.

c. Colour in Samantha. Use the right colours.

2. Draw lines under the adjectives and boxes around the nouns they describe. Join each adjective to the correct noun. The first one is done for you.

Samantha had <u>grey</u> rings around the eyes, a grey bill,

grey legs and grey feet. She was a young silver gull.

3. **a.** Underline the adjectives in the following description.

When silver gulls grow up, parts of them change colour. They now have red rings around the eyes, red bills, red legs and red feet.

b. Colour in Samantha now that she has grown up.

MORE ACTION

- Read the book, *Samantha Seagull's Sandals*. It will be in your class library, school library or district library. Find out what happened to her.
- Think of adjectives to describe a parrot, a kookaburra and a crow. See how many you can find. Write in your own book or folder.

A literary description describes something like a bird, an animal, a person or a scene in an interesting way. You will find literary descriptions in picture books, poems or stories.

15

Text Type:

POETRY

NUMERAL ADJECTIVES

Numeral or **numbering adjectives** tell you the number of things, as in *one* juicy orange. They can also tell in which order things appear, as in the *first* person on the bus.

One Juicy Orange

One juicy orange in a tree,
Two tiny turtles in the sea,
Three yummy pancakes in a heap,
Four lazy leopards, fast asleep,
Five rapid runners in a race,
Six shining sunbeams on my face,
Seven tasty apples in a pie,
Eight soaring spaceships in the sky,
Nine black umbrellas in the rain,
Ten noisy schoolboys on a train.

1. In your own book or folder, write all the numeral adjectives you can find in the poem, *One Juicy Orange*.

2. There are many descriptive adjectives, too. Write them in your own book or folder.

3. Draw boxes around the numeral adjectives which show the order of things. The first one is done for you.

   a. The ⬚first⬚ and second girls won prizes.

   b. This is the third time I have jumped this high.

   c. They were the fourth and fifth students in the line.

   d. He is the sixth player to win the medal.

   e. She won first prize at the Royal Easter Show.

4. Fill in the gaps with numeral adjectives.

a. first, second, _____, _____,
_____, sixth person.

b. One apple, three apples, five apples, _____ apples,
_____ apples.

c. Twelve boys, ten boys, eight boys, _____ boys,
_____ boys, _____boys.

5. Do this numeral adjectives wiggleword.

ACROSS
2. first, second, third, fourth, _____ .
3. _____ blind mice, See how they run.
4. One before fifth _____

DOWN
1. First, second, _____
2. How many eggs? ○ ○ ○ ○ ○
3. One nose, ten toes, _____ eyes.

MORE ACTION

• Read the poem aloud. Find other poems that describe things.

Poetry is a special form of
speaking or writing. The poem, *One Juicy Orange,*
is special because it describes all kinds of different things in an interesting way.
You find poems like this in books of poetry in your school or class library.

Text Type:

INFORMATION REPORT

PERSONAL PRONOUNS

Personal pronouns are words that are used in place of nouns. For example, Emus live in Australia. *They* are big. In the second sentence, They is a personal pronoun. It is used instead of *emus*. The personal pronouns are *I, me, he, him, she, her, it, we, us, you, they and them.*

Emus

Emus live in Australia. They are the second largest birds in the world.
The African Ostrich is taller. It is the largest bird and can grow to more than 200 cm high. Neither bird can fly. Emus have long legs, dark, grey-brown feathers and a grey-blue throat and face. They can run as fast as 48 km per hour. The male emu sits on the eggs and looks after the young emus. He is a very good father. The female does not sit on the eggs. She goes off with her friends.

1. Draw a box around the personal pronouns in this information report. Write them here

_____

2. Finish these sentences with personal pronouns.

   a. The male emu sits on the eggs. _____ is a very good father.

      We should be proud of _____ .

   b. The female emu does not sit on the eggs. _____ goes off with

      her friends. The male emu would not be proud of _____ .

3. Pick from the box to finish these sentences.

> **They   You   them   We   us   them**

Our class went to the zoo. _____ saw some emus. _____ were very tall.

There were five of _____. They were not scared of _____ at all.

_____ should come and see _____, too.

4. Cross out the wrong personal pronouns in these sentences.

a. We saw (they, them) at the zoo.

b. (We, Us) went to see the emus.

c. Tillie and (I, me) were in the bus.

d. (You, Them) should visit the emus.

e. (I, Me) saw the emu sitting on the eggs.

5. Write in a personal pronoun and cross out the noun.

a. I saw Jim. (Jim _____ was sick. (Jim _____) is better now.

b. An emu is a big bird. (An emu _____) can grow to 180 cms.

c. Have you read a book about emus? (Emus _____) are interesting creatures.

MORE ACTION

• Read the book, *Enoch the Emu*. It will be in your class library, school library or district library. Find out what happened to Enoch.

POSSESSIVE PRONOUNS

Possessive pronouns show ownership. They are used in place of nouns, like this: The ball belongs to Ali. It is **his**. We say *his* instead of Ali's. The possessive pronouns are *his, hers, its, mine, ours, yours* and *theirs*.

The Big Coloured Ball

(This is part of a narrative about a big, coloured ball that has a mind of its own.)

"Give it back!" said Barney. "It's mine!"

"It's not yours. It's not!" yelled Julie.
"It's mine! It's mine!"

"Stop that," said Mr Jackson.
"It's not yours, Barney, and it's not yours, Julie. It belongs to everyone in the class. It's theirs."

But the big, coloured ball decided that it was not his, hers or theirs. It rose slowly into the air and floated away.

1. Read through this part of the story and draw a box around every possessive pronoun you can find.

   Remember that *it's* is not a possessive pronoun, but a short way of saying *it is*. Colour in the ball.

2. Write a possessive pronoun to finish each sentence.

   a. Julie said that the ball was _____.

   b. Barney said, "It is _____."

   c. Mr Jackson said that the ball belonged to the class. It was _____.

3. Finish these sentences with the correct possessive pronouns.

    a. You own the bike. It is _____ (yours, mine).

    b. She won the prize. It was _____ (hers, his).

    c. This is the class's work. It is all _____ (its, theirs).

    d. You take the cake. It's _____ (his, yours).

    e. They bought the puppy. Now it's _____ (his, theirs).

4. How many possessive pronouns can you find in this box?
Write them underneath. (If there are two the same, write them twice.)
Read across and down.

S	E	H	E	R	S
T	H	E	I	R	S
O	U	R	S	H	I
H	I	S	R	I	T
M	I	N	E	S	S
T	Y	O	U	R	S

_____

_____

_____

MORE ACTION

• What other adventures did the Big Coloured Ball have? Did it land in the
sea, in a jungle, on a space ship or did it go to another planet?
Make up your own narrative. Write in your own book.

A narrative tells a story.
It contains things that happen to the characters
and often has a surprise ending. You will read, see and hear
narratives in books, at the movies, and on television.

ACTION VERBS

Action verbs are doing words like *jump*, *run* or *talk*.

How to Get to Town

Take these things
Money for train ticket and shopping.
A sun hat

Method
Cross the road.
Run to the station.
Buy your train ticket.
Catch the train.
Sit near a window.
Read a book.
Leave the train at Town Hall.

1. Write down all the action verbs you can find in this procedure. The first two are done for you.

Get, take, _____

_____

2. Finish the action verbs. Pick from the box.

a. S_____ onto the train.

b. W_____ in line.

c. C_____ the stairs.

d. O_____ the window.

e. M_____ away from the door.

| Climb |
| Open |
| Step |
| Move |
| Wait |

3. Use each of these action verbs in a sentence. The first one is done for you.

a. run ___I run to the station._____

b. sit _____

c. read _____

d. climb _____

e. buy _____

4. Here are some other ways to get to town. Finish the action verbs.

Pick from the box.

Fly   Ride   Catch   Row   Walk

R_____ a bike.

W_____ with Dad.

R_____ a boat.

F_____ a plane.

C_____ a bus.

MORE ACTION

• In your own book, write your own procedure for cooking sausages or some
other food on the barbecue.

• Pick out the action verbs in your procedure.
Draw a circle around them.

SAYING, THINKING AND FEELING VERBS

Doing words like *shout* or *whisper* are **saying verbs**; doing words like *think* or *wonder* are **thinking verbs**; doing words like *love* or *hate* are **feeling verbs.**

Goldilocks and the Three Bears

Goldilocks visited the bears' house.
She ate Baby Bear's porridge, broke his
chair and went to sleep in his bed.
The bears came home and found her.
I think she was lucky to escape.

1. Cross out the wrong verbs.

   a. The bears (wondered, thought, knew) who had been eating their porridge.

   b. They (knew, imagined, wondered) who it was when they found Goldilocks.

   c. Goldilocks must have (whispered, spoken, yelled) loudly when she saw the three bears.

   d. Goldilocks just (hated, loved, disliked) Baby Bear's porridge.

   e. I (think, wonder, doubt) Goldilocks was lucky to escape.

2. Write these verbs in the correct boxes.

   dislike   think   hate   whisper   wonder   know   chatter   tell   adore

SAYING	THINKING	FEELING

3. Write in a word to complete each sentence. Pick from the box.

thought	love	shouted	recited	whispered

a. We _____ so as not to wake the baby.

b. I _____ it was a very good idea.

c. We really _____ playing on the beach.

d. I _____ so everyone could hear.

e. They _____ the poem in class.

4. Finish these sentences with your own words.

a. I dislike _____

_____ .

b. I love _____

_____ .

c. I whispered _____

_____ .

d. I wondered _____

_____ .

e. I yelled _____

_____ .

MORE ACTION

• What else happened at the bears' house? Write three things in your own book. Underline the verbs.

A personal response sums up
what a story is about. It gives your opinion, too.
You make personal responses to stories you hear, see and read.

25

Text Type:

NARRATIVE

ADVERBS

Adverbs usually add meaning to verbs. They tell us *how*, *when* and *where* things are done. For example, He ran *quickly* (how); I went *yesterday* (when). They came *here* (where). Adverbs usually add meaning to verbs.

Spooky Night

It was raining heavily, the wind was blowing wildly and I was really scared. Then I heard a noise. Something was coming slowly up the stairs. My heart was beating loudly so I opened the door to run quickly into Mum's room. Then I saw the cat sitting quietly on the top stair, carefully licking her paws. She had come in out of the rain.

1. There are many adverbs that tell "how" something happened in this short narrative. The first one is *heavily*. It tells us how it was raining. Underline all the adverbs that tell how

(Hint: In this narrative they all end with "ly".)

2. Finish these sentences with an adverb that tells how. Pick from the box.

carefully	**quickly**	**softly**	**slowly**	**safely**

a. We looked both ways and crossed the road _____.

b. Shh! Speak _____ or you will frighten the birds.

c. She ran _____ and won the race.

d. Chew your food _____.

e. Think _____ before you answer.

3. Draw boxes around the adverbs that tell "when" in these sentences. The first one is done for you.

a. I went swimming yesterday , today and I will go tomorrow.

b. I will see you later, not now.

c. He will be here soon.

d. We will be there early.

e. They will be our friends always.

4. Draw boxes around the adverbs that tell "where". The first one is done for you.

a. He fell over .

b. Come here, John!

c. It is there, on the table.

d. You will find their house nearby.

e. He fell down.

f. She ran alongside.

g. Ian walked underneath.

h. The balloon went up.

i. Come inside!

j. You can play outside.

5. Write in an adverb.

a. This cow is walking _____.

b. This plane is flying _____.

c. This girl is thinking _____.

d. This boy is eating _____.

e. They were sitting _____.

MORE ACTION

• In your own book or folder, write as many "ly" adverbs as you can find.

A narrative tells a story.
It contains things that happen to the
characters and often has a surprise ending. You will read, see
and hear narratives in books, at the movies, on the radio and on television.

REVISION: UNITS 1-9

1. Underline the **common nouns** and draw boxes around the **proper nouns** in these sentences.

   a. Jenny Smith went to the beach in the bus and saw the boats.

   b. Cam saw birds, surfers and dogs at Bondi.

   c. Mrs O'Toole took Chan and Jason to Kakadu.

2. Underline the **descriptive adjectives** and draw boxes around the **numeral adjectives** in these sentences.

   a. Seven tasty apples in a pie and eight soaring spaceships were in the poem.

   b. Five fat flounder were swimming in the salty sea.

   c. Ten tables and ten tiny chairs were in the two toy shops.

3. Fill in the **personal pronouns**.

   a. Mary is fun. _____ always makes me laugh.

   b. My father is strong. _____ can pick me up easily.

   c. We saw the koalas. I really like _____.

   d. The birds are nesting. _____ have laid their eggs.

   e. My name is Carlos. _____ am team captain.

4. Underline the **possessive pronouns**.

   a. That's yours, that's mine and that's hers.

   b. He said that the big ball was his, but Mr Jackson said that it was theirs.

5. Draw boxes around the **action verbs**.

    a. The children run, jump, paddle and swim.

    b. Run, run and win!

    c. Read a book and eat an apple every day.

6. Write down the **saying verbs** in these sentences.

    a. I whispered to Robyn. _____

    b. They shouted at us. _____

    c. "Don't chatter," our teacher said. _____

7. Underline the **adverbs**.

    a. It was raining heavily and the wind was blowing wildly.

    b. We ran quickly to the train yesterday to get home early.

8. Fill in the spaces with adverbs from the box.

loudly	softly	quickly

    a. We ran _____ and won the race.

    b. I shouted _____ so they could hear.

    c. They whispered _____ to me.

9. Draw boxes around the verbs and circles around the adverbs.

    a. The girls played the piano beautifully.

    b. The boys planted the tree carefully.

NONE WRONG (excellent)	☐	1-2 WRONG (good)	☐	3-4 WRONG (pass)	☐	5 OR MORE WRONG (more work needed)	☐

PREPOSITIONS

Prepositions are words like *in, on* or *at* that you find at the beginning of groups of words called phrases. They often tell you the position or place of things. Here are some examples: *in* the soup, *on* the table and *at* the picnic. Some other common prepositions are *near, beside, over, from, onto, through, above* and *with*. There are many others.

The Best Boiled Eggs

You need

2 or more fresh eggs

a small saucepan

water

Method

Take the eggs from the refrigerator.
Place them in the saucepan.
Cover the eggs with water.
Bring the eggs to the boil.
Boil on low heat for 3 minutes.

Take the eggs from the water.
Place them in egg cups.
Serve with toast cut into pieces.
Yum!

1. Fill in the spaces with prepositions from *The Best Boiled Eggs*.

a. _____ the refrigerator

b. _____ water

c. _____ low heat

d. _____ the water

e. _____ toast

f. _____ the saucepan

g. _____ the boil

h. _____ three minutes

i. _____ egg cups

j. _____ pieces

2. Think of prepositions to fill these spaces. Write them in the spaces.

   a. I like to dip pieces of toast _____ my egg.

   b. Break the shell _____ a knife or spoon.

   c. Sprinkle salt _____ the egg.

   d. I like to spread egg _____ my toast.

   e. We like hard-boiled eggs _____ sandwiches.

3. Use these prepositions to make phrases. The first one is done for you.

   The phrases do not have to be about eggs.

   on ___the___ ___table___,   in _____ _____ ,

   at _____ _____ ,   near _____ _____ ,

   over _____ _____ ,   beside _____ _____ ,

   onto _____ _____ ,   underneath _____ _____ ,

   outside _____ _____ ,   against _____ _____ .

4. Join the words to a picture to make a phrase. Write the word.

   in a _____

   under a _____

   over a _____

   on a _____

   with my _____

MORE ACTION

• Have a preposition hunt on a page of a book you are reading.
  See who can find the most.

A procedure tells you how
to do or make something. In it you will find things
you need and steps that tell you what to do. You will find procedures in
recipes, rules of games, gardening books, books on how to make things and travel books.

Text Type:

FACTUAL RECOUNT

CONJUNCTIONS

Conjunctions are joining words. They join parts of what we say and write, like Jack *and* Jill or We went fishing *but* we didn't catch anything.

Fishing

I went fishing with Dad and my friend, Louisa. We found a good spot and Dad threw out our lines for us. We did try to but they kept getting tangled. I had a bite and a big tug on my line but the fish got away. We fished for a long time but didn't catch anything. I said, "Let's buy our fish next time," and Dad said, "We'll try again next week."

1. Read this recount and draw a box around all the *and* and *but* conjunctions.

2. Fill in the gaps with *and* or *but* conjunctions.

   a. I like fish _____ chips.

   b. We went fishing _____ we didn't catch anything.

   c. Louisa _____ I went with Dad.

   d. I had a bite _____ the fish got away.

   e. Dad _____ I will go fishing again next week.

3. *Because, unless* and *although* are three more conjunctions. Fill in each gap, using one of these words.

a. You cannot go _____ you finish your work.

b. I will win _____ I have been training.

c. _____ he is small, he is a very fast runner.

d. _____ it rains, we will go to the beach.

e. He cannot go fishing by himself _____ he is too young.

4. Join the sentences using one of these conjunctions. Write on the lines.

because   and   but   because   unless

a. I am seven. Louisa is too.

_____

b. I tried. I didn't catch anything.

_____

c. We went home. The fish did not bite.

_____

d. I am keen to go again. It was fun.

_____

e. It is fun at the beach. It is raining.

_____

MORE ACTION

• *When, if* and *while* are more conjunctions. In your own book or folder, write sentences with these conjunctions in them.

A factual recount tells us about something that happened in the past. The events are described in order, one after another. You will find factual recounts in books about the past, on television, in films and in much of the writing you do yourself.

12

Text Type:

EXPLANATION

ARTICLES

There are three **articles**, *a*, *an*, and *the*, as in *a* delicious fruit, *an* apple and *the* juice. Use *the* if the noun described is the only one as in *the* best book. Use *an* instead of *a* if the following noun starts with a vowel (a, e, i, o, u) as in *an* apple. You will also find that the correct one sounds right.

Why Apples are Good for You

Apples are good for you.
It is said that "an apple a day keeps the doctor away"… and this is why.
Apples contain a number of important vitamins and minerals.
The juice, the skin and the flesh are good for the stomach.
The skin is good for the teeth, too. It is "nature's toothbrush".
An apple is a non-fattening fruit and a delicious snack.
Eat an apple right away!

1. This explanation has many articles in it. Draw a box around every one.

2. Fill in the articles.

a. I like to eat _____ apple in _____ morning.

b. _____ orange is _____ good food, too.

c. _____ boys and _____ girls in our class always have

_____ apple for lunch.

d. Would you like _____apple or _____ peach?

e. I would like _____ apricot, _____ banana and _____

ripest pear in _____ white box.

3. Join the correct articles to words on the right. Sometimes two articles will do. The first one is done for you.

a ———————————————————————— juicy pineapple

ripest apple

orange drink

an apple pie

biggest mango

bunch of grapes

peach pie

the navel orange

4. Fill in the articles to finish these playground rhymes.

a. I saw you in _____ ocean.

I saw you in _____ sea.

I saw you in _____ bathtub.

Whoops! Pardon me!

b. There's music in _____ horseshoe,

There's music in _____ nail,

There's music in _____ tomcat,

If you only pull his tail.

MORE ACTION

• Write an explanation why too much take away is bad for you.
Write in your own book or folder.

An explanation explains how
something works or why something is like
it is, such as *Why Apples are Good for You.* You will find
explanations in books, on film, on television and in some videos.

35

NOUN GROUP

A **noun group** is a group of words, usually based on a noun, as in *a bottlenose dolphin*. Sometimes a noun group can be only one word as in *Danny* is big.

Danny Dolphin

Danny Dolphin is a bottlenose dolphin. He has a big mouth with tiny teeth. He can catch big and little fish in his open mouth. Danny is called a bottlenose dolphin because his mouth is like a long nose and it looks like a bottle.

1. Fill in these noun groups from the description of Danny Dolphin.

a. a _____ dolphin

b. his _____ mouth

c. a _____ nose

d. big and _____ fish

e. a big mouth _____ _____ teeth.

2. Write down the two noun groups from this sentence.

Danny Dolphin is a bottlenose dolphin.

_____

_____

3. Add words to these noun groups to make them bigger. Pick from the boxes.

a.   **big**   **bottlenose**   **a**   **friendly**

                                                           dolphin

                                             _____ dolphin

                          _____ _____ dolphin

             _____ _____ _____ dolphin

       _____ _____ _____ dolphin

b.   **wide**   **a**   **big**   **open**   **an**

                                                           mouth

                                             _____ mouth

                        _____ _____ mouth

             _____ _____ _____ mouth

       _____ _____ _____ mouth

c.   **tiny**   **twenty**   **Danny's**   **top**

                                                   teeth

                                     _____ teeth

                         _____ _____ teeth

             _____ _____ _____ teeth

       _____ _____ _____ _____ teeth

MORE ACTION

• Make these noun groups longer.

_____ _____ whale, _____ _____ penguin

_____ _____ albatross

ADVERBIAL PHRASES

Adverbial phrases are groups of words that do the work of an adverb. They tell how *(with their wings)* when *(in the spring)* and where *(in the water)*. They begin with a preposition and end with a noun or pronoun.

Birds

Most birds can fly through the air. They live in trees, on cliffs or among sand dunes near the sea. Some birds fly over the ocean and catch fish by diving under the waves. They build their nests in spring by picking up twigs and other materials with their beaks or with their feet.

1. This part of an information report about birds has many adverbial phrases in it. Complete the ones below by writing in the prepositions from this report.

a. _____ the air

b. _____ cliffs

c. _____ the sea

d. _____ the waves

e. _____ their beaks

f. _____ trees

g. _____ sand dune

h. _____ the ocean

i. _____ spring

j. _____ their feet

2. Write a preposition to finish each phrase. Pick from the box.

a. Some birds eat worms. Worms live _____ the ground.

b. Some birds live _____ the seashore.

c. Birds lay eggs _____ spring.

d. Eagles catch their prey _____ their talons.

e. The parent birds sit _____ the eggs.

on
under
at
with
in

3. Put each adverbial phrase into a sentence. Begin with these words.

a. through the air   Birds _____

_____

b. during the night   Most birds _____

_____

c. along the beach   Seagulls _____

_____

d. with their feet   Ducks _____

_____

e. in the frozen regions   Penguins _____

_____

4. Do this bird wiggleword.

ACROSS

2. Baby birds live _____ the nest.

3. Birds fly _____ the air.

5. Owls hunt _____ dark.

DOWN

1. Worms live _____ ground.

3. You will see birds if you go _____ the beach.

4. The albatross flies _____ the sea.

MORE ACTION

• Find out more about birds. Write about them in your own book.
  How many adverbial phrases did you write?

An information report gives you facts about
things such as birds, fish, planets or African animals.
You will find information reports in books, films, videos and television.

39

TAKE A TEST 2

REVISION: UNITS 10-14

1. Circle the prepositions in the following:

on the table,   under the chair,   near the creek,

over the moon,   through the gate.

2. Fill in the spaces with prepositions. Pick from the box.

in	behind	over

a. I jumped _____ the hurdle.

b. We swam _____ the pool.

c. She hid _____ the bush.

3. Finish these sentences.

a. Conjunctions are _____ words.

They _____ parts of sentences.

b. Write conjunctions in these spaces.

Jack _____ Jill,   fun _____ games,

fish _____ chips.

We took our lunch _____ forgot our drinks.

Clean your teeth _____ brush your hair.

4. Underline the articles.

a. An apple a day keeps the doctor away.

b. A dog is an interesting pet.

5. Fill in the correct articles.

She is _____ best player. We had _____ apple for lunch.

He is _____ kind person.

6. Finish these noun groups with words from the box.

long	little	bottlenose	open

a _____ dolphin,

his _____ mouth,   a _____ nose,

big and _____ fish.

7. Underline the noun groups.

a. A tiny fish was eaten by the hungry dolphin.

b. Two dolphins played clever tricks.

8. Underline the adverbial phrases. The first one is done for you.
(It is easy if you find the prepositions *in, with* and *through* first.)

a. Birds fly <u>through the air.</u>   c. They build their nests in spring.

b. They live in trees.   d. They pick up twigs with their beaks.

9. Finish the adverbial phrases with prepositions. Pick from the box.

under	in	on

a. We sat _____ the bench.

b. I swam _____ the pool.

c. We hid _____ the table.

Text Type:

POETRY

SENTENCES

A **sentence** makes sense by itself. Two types of sentences are: the statement, as in *I have seen the bees.* and the question, as in *Have you seen the trees?*

The Bees' Knees

Have you seen the forest?
Have you seen the trees?
Have you seen the butterflies?
Have you seen the bees?

I have seen the forest.
I have seen the trees.
I have seen the butterflies.
I have seen the bees.

Well, have you seen their knees?

1. a. How many sentences are there in this poem? _____

   b. How many statements? _____ *(Hint: All statements finish with a full stop.)*

   c. How many questions? _____ *(Hint: All questions are followed by a question mark)*

2. Finish these sentences with words from the box.

   a. Bees give us _____ to eat.

   b. Bees have _____ legs.

   c. Bees can _____.

   d. Bees live in _____.

   e. Bees make a _____ sound.

   | six |
   | buzzing |
   | sting |
   | hives |
   | honey |

3. Draw lines to match up the sentences parts. The first one is done for you.

a. I saw the bees   honey?

b. Have you been   flowers.

c. Do you like eating   buzz?

d. A bee is an   stung by a bee?

e. Bees visit   insect.

f. Do bees   in the hive.

4. In your own book or folder, make these jumbled words into a sentence.
(Hint: Remember to start each one with a capital letter and end it with a full stop or question mark.)

a. hives in live bees

b. visit like to bees flowers

c. buzzing you the can hear bees

d. in trees the are forest the

e. knees bees do have

5. Add your ending to complete these sentences.

a. Bees are _____ .

b. The bees make _____ .

c. A beehive is _____ .

MORE ACTION

• Find out more about bees. Write down what you find.
  Have you written statements or questions?

Poetry is a special form of
speaking or writing. It can do many things such as
painting word pictures, telling a story or describing feelings. It can rhyme but it
does not have to. It can be funny, too. You will find poetry in books, in newspapers and on signs in the street.

EXCLAMATIONS

Exclamations are sentences or parts of sentences that show strong feeling, such as *Yeow!* They must be followed by an exclamation mark.

The Snake

"Look out!" I yelled. "It will bite you!"
"Jump, Julie! Jump!"

The black snake was on the path straight in front of Julie. She had not seen it at first.

"Yeow!" she screamed, and jumped away from the danger. I grabbed her arm and pulled her on to the rock.

"Wow!" she said. "That was close."

1. Write down the exclamations from this part of a narrative. You do not have to write the speech marks.

_____

_____

2. Write exclamation marks after the exclamations and full stops or question marks after the others.

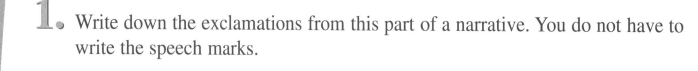

Hooray   We've won   Let's go   I don't want any, thank

What a cold day   Where are you going   Yum, yum

We sat very still   Ouch   Where's my coat

3. Write the correct words in the speech bubbles. Put in the exclamation marks. Colour in the pictures.

YUM YUM	**HE'S WON**
BE CAREFUL	**WOW, IT'S COLD**

a.

b.

c.

d.

MORE ACTION

• In your own book, write what you might say if you hurt your foot, you won a race, you opened a wonderful birthday present, or you were told to eat your least favourite vegetable.

Text Type:

PROCEDURE

COMMANDS

Commands are sentences that tell someone what to do. They are orders or instructions, such as *Swim between the flags*. They finish with a full stop or in some cases an exclamation mark, such as *Get out of the water!* (There's a shark.)

How to be Safe at the Beach

You will need
- *Your swim suit, board shorts or bikini*
- *A beach umbrella*
- *Towel*
- *A beach hat*
- *T-shirt*
- *Thongs or sandals*
- *Sunscreen*

How to be safe
- *Wear your beach hat.*
- *Put on sunscreen.*
- *Sit under a beach umbrella when not swimming.*
- *Swim between the flags.*
- *Swim with Mum or Dad.*
- *Put on T-shirt after swimming.*
- *Keep near the shore.*
- *Have a great time!*

1. Write down what you think are the two most important commands for beach safety in the procedure, *How to be Safe at the Beach.*

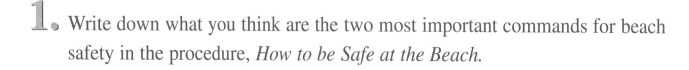

_____

_____

2. Write commands in the speech bubbles. Pick from the box or write your own. Finish each command with a full stop or exclamation mark.

PUT ON SOME SUNSCREEN	**GET THAT HAT ON**
SWIM BETWEEN THE FLAGS	**COME OUT OF THE SUN**

a.

b.

c.

d.

MORE ACTION

- Colour in the pictures. Write more commands to go with them.

  Write in your own book.

CLAUSES

Clauses are groups of words about some sort of action, such as *He shakes hands with me.* Clauses usually have a verb (a doing, being or having word), such as *shakes,* and a subject, such as *He.* Sometimes a clause can be a whole sentence, such as *Biffo is my dog,* or it can be part of a sentence, such as … *because he biffs other dogs.*

My Dog Biffo

Biffo is my dog. He is a mixture. He has a black ear and a brown ear. His back is brown and black, too. We call him Biffo because he biffs other dogs if they growl and bark at me. Biffo is my friend. I like him and he likes me.

1. Finish these clauses from My Dog Biffo.

a. Biffo _____ _____ dog.

b. He _____ _____ mixture.

c. His back _____ _____ and _____, too.

d. We call him _____

e. because he _____ _____ dogs

f. if they _____ _____ me.

g. I _____ him

h. and he _____ me.

2. A principal clause is the main clause in a sentence. Match these parts to make principal clauses. The first one is done for you.

Biffo	has two pets at her place.
Do you know	like my dog, Biffo.
I	are good pets.
Dogs	why we call him Biffo?
My friend, Maria	is my friend.
He has	a black ear and a brown ear.

3. A subordinate (dependent) clause cannot make sense by itself. Match the principal clauses to the subordinate clauses on the right. The first one is done for you.

We call him Biffo	after he has had his dinner.
He is a mixture	because he has different coloured ears.
Biffo fights other dogs	if we look after them.
Dogs make good pets	when he is hungry.
I feed Biffo	because he biffs other dogs.
I take Biffo for a walk	who growl and bark at me.

4. Finish these principal clauses in your own book or folder. Use your own words.

a. Dogs are . . . . b. We like . . . . c. My pet is a . . . .

d. I wish I had . . . . e. My friend Jock's pets are . . . .

MORE ACTION

• Find the main (principal) clauses in a page of a book you are reading.
• Write your own factual description of your pet.
  How many clauses can you find in it?

A factual description describes a particular thing, such as a particular pet. You will find factual descriptions in books, films, videos, on television and in your own writing.

Text Type:
EXPOSITION

COMPOUND SENTENCES

A **compound sentence** is made up of two or more clauses joined by the conjunctions *and* or *but*. An example is *We think our team is best* and *we are proud of it*. Each clause is a principal clause. It makes sense by itself.

Our Team is Best

Our netball team is the best team in the school and it is the best team in the whole district. Our team does win competitions, but we are good sports, too.

We always shake hands with the other team after a game and we clap them if they play well. Our coach tells us to be good winners and she tells us to be good losers as well.

We think our team is fast and we are proud of it.

1. Finish these compound sentences from *Our Team is Best*.

a. Our team is the best team in the school and _____

_____

b. Our team does win competitions, but _____

_____

c. We always shake hands with the other team after a game and _____

_____

d. Our coach tells us to be good winners and _____

_____

2. **a.** How many compound sentences can you find in *Our Team is Best?* ☐

  b. How many principal clauses are in *Our Team is Best?* (There are two principal clauses in each compound sentence in the exposition.) ☐

  c. **(i)** Write down one compound sentence from *Our Team is Best.*

  _____

  _____

  (ii) Write down one principal clause. _____

  _____

3. Finish these compound sentences. Use your own words.

  a. It is good to win but _____

  _____ .

  b. I like to play _____ and _____

  _____ .

4. In your own book or folder, make up compound sentences about this picture. Use *and* or *but*.

MORE ACTION

• Write your own argument about your team, class or school. Say why it is the best.

Text Type:

NARRATIVE

COHESION: HOLDING TEXTS TOGETHER

Texts are held together in many ways. One is using words again and again, as in *the Gingerbread Man … the Gingerbread Man*. Another one is using a different word to mean the same person or thing, as in *The Gingerbread Man* laughed. *He* ran on. This process is called cohesion.

The Gingerbread Man

"Stop!" mooed the cow. "Stop, Gingerbread Man!
I want to eat you up."
The Gingerbread Man laughed. He ran past her
and shouted:
"Run, run, run, as fast as you can.
You can't catch me, I'm the Gingerbread Man."

1. **a.** This is part of the story of the Gingerbread Man. Underline every time *Gingerbread Man* is used, and join them all up.

b. Write three other words that are used instead of *the Gingerbread Man*.

y_____,   H_____,   m_____.

2. Write in the missing words that hold the following text together. Pick from the box.

him	them	he	they	her	He	him

a. The old woman and the old man ran after the Gingerbread Man but

_____ could not catch _____.

b. The Gingerbread Man ran away. _____ was too fast for _____

c. The cow had tried to catch _____ but _____

was too fast for_____, too.

3. Draw a Gingerbread Man in this box. Colour him in and finish the following sentences with linking words from the box.

him	you	he
him	He	

a. This is the Gingerbread Man. _____ is brown and delicious.

I would like to eat _____ , wouldn't _____?

b. The wily fox tricked the Gingerbread Man. How did _____ trick _____?

4. Read this little poem. Which three words are repeated many times? How many times is each one repeated. Write the numbers in the boxes.

_____   _____   _____

☐   ☐   ☐

POPCORN
Pop the popcorn
Pop the popcorn
Pop it in the pot.
Pop the popcorn
Pop the popcorn
See the popcorn pop.
Eat the popcorn hot.

MORE ACTION

• Read the story of the *The Gingerbread Man.*
What happened to him?

This is part of the story of *The Gingerbread Man.* It is a famous traditional story, a narrative. It contains many characters and tells us what happens to the Gingerbread Man. You will find traditional stories in collections of stories. Look in your school library.

Text Type:
REVIEW

SYNONYMS AND ANTONYMS

Synonyms are words with similar meanings, like *big* and *large*. **Antonyms** are words with opposite meanings, like *good* and *bad*. Synonyms and antonyms help to make your writing more interesting and form cohesive links in texts.

The Hobbit

Dad has been reading me The Hobbit by J.R.R. Tolkien, a really exciting book. I think it is absolutely fabulous and I love hearing some of it each night. It is about good and imaginary creatures and fantastic adventures. The hero is Bilbo Baggins, a hobbit; Gandalf, a mighty wizard . . . and, of course, the horrifying Gollum. You just have to read this book.

1. Circle your favourite synonym (word with similar meaning) in each of the following descriptions.

a. a strong,
    mighty   wizard
    powerful

b. a dreadful
    horrible   dragon
    vile

c. Full of good
    marvellous   adventures
    terrific
    wonderful

d. an exciting
    thrilling   book
    interesting

e. an outstanding
    exceptional   story
    excellent

f. I like
    love   hearing it
    adore
    enjoy

2. Join up the antonyms (the words with opposite meanings).
The first one is done for you.

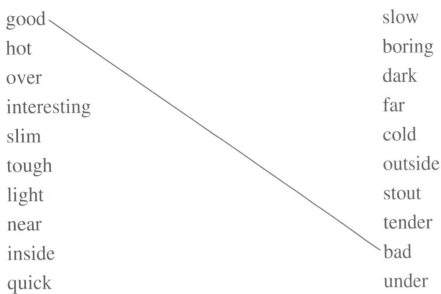

good	slow
hot	boring
over	dark
interesting	far
slim	cold
tough	outside
light	stout
near	tender
inside	bad
quick	under

3. How many words can you find in this pattern that mean HAPPY. Write them down.

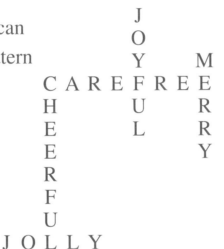

How many?

_____

_____

4. Write a sentence containing one of the above words e.g. joyful or carefree.

_____

MORE ACTION

• Find as many synonyms (words of similar meaning) for these words as you can. Use a thesaurus to help you:

　　eat, 　*beautiful,* 　*wet.*

CONNECTIVES

Connectives are "signal words". They join up sentences and tell us what is coming next. Examples are *next* and *last*.

Eggshell Mosaic

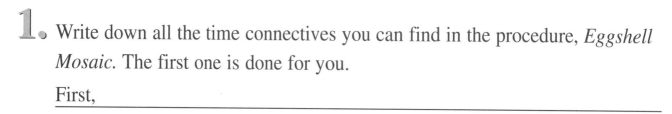

You will need
2 empty eggshells
1 piece of white paper
1 box of paints, glue

Method
First, paint the empty eggshells.
Then, let them dry.
Next, break the shells into pieces.
Now, draw a picture on the paper
(a cat, dog, bird, person).
Afterwards, brush some glue on the paper.
Finally, stick pieces of eggshell on the glued paper.
Now you have an eggshell mosaic!

1. Write down all the time connectives you can find in the procedure, *Eggshell Mosaic*. The first one is done for you.

First, _____

2. Write connectives in the spaces. Pick from the box.
How to Make a Different Eggshell Mosaic.

> **Finally**
> **First of all**
> **Next**

a. _____ , use a piece of coloured paper.

b. _____ , do exactly what you did before.

c. _____ , you have a different eggshell mosaic.

3. Imagine that you are having your lunch. Write what you would do, using these connectives.

To begin, I _____

_____.

Next, I _____

_____.

After that, I _____

_____.

Last of all, I _____

_____.

4. Fill in the empty spaces with connectives from the box.

Going To School

now	Next	Then	To begin

_____ I get dressed. _____ I have

my breakfast and clean my teeth. _____ I pack my

school bag and _____ I'm ready to go.

MORE ACTION

- In your own book or folder, write what you do when you are getting ready to go to a party. Use as many connectives as you can.

A procedure tells you how to do or make something. In it you will find the things you need and the steps that show you what to do. You will find procedures in recipes, rules of games, books on how to make things, gardening books and travel books.

REVISION: UNITS 15-22

1. Write down a statement, a question and an exclamation from this paragraph.

Bees like flowers. Did you know that bees can sting? Look out! I still like bees, though.

Statement _____

Question _____

Exclamation _____

2. Write punctuation marks at the end of each sentence.

a. Where is your book   **d.** Give me that pencil

b. Look out   **e.** Where is your mother

c. I like tomato sandwiches

3. Underline two commands from the following:

I wear a sun hat at the beach. Put on your sunscreen.

Put on your T-shirt, now. Have you brought it?

4. Underline two principal clauses.

in his kennel,   My dog Biffo is clever.

I take him for a walk. a black ear and a brown ear.

5. Join these principal clauses to make compound sentences. The first one is done for you.

Our team wins   and eat good food.

We train hard   and we are proud of it.

We think our team is best   and we play fairly.

6. Write in the missing pronouns that hold these sentences together.

| him | He | him | they |

a. The Gingerbread Man was cheeky. _____ ran away.

b. The old woman and the old man chased the Gingerbread Man but

_____ could not catch _____.

c. The fox ate the Gingerbread Man because he tricked _____.

7. Pick from the box to write two words of similar meaning (synonyms) beside these words.

| love | vile | quick | speedy | adore | ghastly |

a. horrible _____   _____

b. fast _____   _____

c. like _____   _____

8. Fill in the correct words. Pick from the box.

| Then, | Finally, | First, |

a. _____ you paint the eggshells.

b. _____ you let them dry.

c. _____ you stick eggshells on the paper.

| NONE WRONG (excellent) | ☐ | 1-2 WRONG (good) | ☐ | 3-4 WRONG (pass) | ☐ | 5 OR MORE WRONG (more work needed) | ☐ |

USING WORDS WELL

It is important to use words correctly when we speak and write. Always speak with correct grammar and check your own writing for errors.

Letter to Mum

Hi Mum!

I'm having a super time here. (Me, My) friend Carlos is great fun. Yesterday we (seen, saw) some dolphins and I (did, done) (my, me) best to get you a photo.

Carlos and (I, me) go swimming every day. (Wear, We're) coming home next Monday.

See (ya, you) then,

Love,

Ronno

PS (Your, You're) still (me, my) best friend. XXX OOO

1. Read through *Letter to Mum* and cross out the incorrect words.

2. Write *did* or *done* in the spaces.

    a. I _____ my work.

    b. They have _____ well.

    c. We _____ the gardening with Dad.

    d. I have _____ the writing.

    e. You _____ a good job.

3. Write *saw* or *seen* in the spaces.

a. They _____ the movie

b. I have _____ it, too.

c. Have you _____ it?

d. I _____ the dolphins.

e. She has _____ the show.

4. Write *sing* or *sung* in the spaces.

a. I _____ in the choir.

b. We have_____ two songs.

c. Have you _____ a duet?

d. Our school has _____ at assembly.

e. They _____ very well.

5. Do this mini-wiggleword.

ACROSS

1. I (done, did) it.
2. They have (saw, seen) them.
3. I (rung, rang) her yesterday.

DOWN

1. Have you (did, done) the work?
2. She (sung, sang) beautifully.

MORE ACTION

• Write a short letter to your mum or dad, telling her or him about something interesting that happened at school. Check it carefully for errors in grammar.

A factual recount tells us about something that happened in the past. Events are described, one after another. You will find factual recounts in books and in your own writing.

Text Type:

FACTUAL
DESCRIPTION

COMPOUND WORDS

Compound words are made up of two smaller words as in *classroom* or *bookshelf*.

Our Classroom

In our classroom there are so many interesting things: an eggshell mosaic on the pegboard and a chart of our best handwriting and art.
There is a chalkboard at the front, cupboards along the walls, bookshelves, computers and computer keyboards.
Our teacher, Mrs Raindrop, is always there and so is my best friend, Jenny Hardcastle. They're both friendly.

1. Circle all the compound words in this factual description.

2. Write them here and write the two smaller words that make them up. The first one is done for you.

classroom	class	room

3. Outside in the playground there are more compound words. Join up the parts to make the new word. Write the words underneath. The first one is done for you.

play   keeper
goal   light
sun   time
play   side
out   ground

playground, _____

_____

4. For lunch we like to have many different fruits. Finish these compound words with the words from the box. Write the words underneath.

melon   fruit   berry   apple   fruit   berry

pine _____   straw _____

passion _____   water _____

grape_____   black _____

_____

_____

_____

MORE ACTION

• Write a factual description of your classroom. How many compound words did you use?

A factual description
describes a particular thing, such as a
particular classroom or a particular animal. You will find
factual descriptions in books, films, videos, on television and in your own writing.

Text Type:

DISCUSSION

HOMONYMS

Homonyms are words that usually have different spellings but sound the same, such as *wear* (Wear a coat.) and *where* (Where is he?) They have different meanings, as you can see. Because they sound the same, they are also called **homophones**. We have to be very careful to use the correct word when we write.

School Uniforms

(Some, sum) people think we should (wear, where) school uniforms because they are neat and (knot, not) (two, too, to) (dear, deer) to (by, buy). Others think we should (not, knot) (where, wear) school uniforms because children should (bee, be) able (too, two, to) dress the (weigh, way) they want (two, too, to).

(There, Their) are really (too, two, to) (weighs, ways) to look at it.

1. Read this part of a discussion on school uniforms. There are many homonyms in it. Cross out the wrong words in the brackets.

2. Cross out the wrong words in these sentences.

   a. Children look (know, no) different in school uniforms.

   b. We have (been, bean) discussing school uniforms.

   c. I like to (chews, choose) what clothes I wear.

   d. Mum (nose, knows) what I like.

   e. (Hour, Our) school uniform is very smart.

3. Put each of these words in a sentence. Write a sentence for each one. The first two are done for you.

    raw, roar;   see, sea;   nose, knows;   hear, here.

I like raw carrots. _____

Listen to that lion roar. _____

_____

_____

_____

_____

_____

_____

4. Write homonyms of these words. The first one is done for you.

there	so	bean	pour
their	____	____	____
see	blue	sent	ate
____	____	____	____
shore	four	hear	road
____	____	____	____

MORE ACTION

• Think of other points in an argument for and against school uniforms. Have a discussion at school or at home.

• Write down some of these points. Can you find some words that could be made into homonyms?

A discussion gives two sides of an argument. You will hear discussions in the playground, in school and at home. You will find discussions in books, too.

Text Type:

POETRY

STARTING SOUNDS AND RHYMES

In poetry and some other writing, the **starting sounds** of words are repeated like the "s" sound in *Simon's singlet* or the "m" sound in *Miss Muffet*. **Rhymes** are found at the ends of words. A sound or a number of sounds are repeated like "ite" and "ight" in *white* and *night* or "im" in *swim* and *him*. Starting sounds and rhymes give special effects in poetry.

Simon's Singlet

Simon's special singlet
Had stripes of green and white.
Simon liked his singlet;
He wore it day and night.

When Simon tried to slip it off
To go in for a swim,
He found his special singlet
Had become a part of him.

1. **a.** Read the poem, *Simon's Singlet*. Circle all the "s" sounds at the beginnings of words.

   b. Draw boxes around each pair of words that rhyme.

   c. Colour in Simon's singlet.

2. Write down the letters that make the starting sounds in the following.
   six slithery snakes,   five funny frogs,   my magnificent mum,
Peter Porter's pet python,   big, brown brawny boys.

_____   _____   _____   _____   _____

3. Fill in the words to make these poems rhyme.
Pick from the box.

Mouse is One

Mouse is one

And mice is two,

Or three or four or more.

You must admit

You've never met

a mice _____.

Chew It Up

Chew it up

and down it goes,

down and down

right to your _____.

4. Match the words that rhyme. The first one is done you.

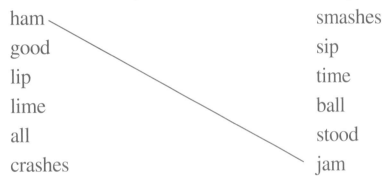

ham	smashes
good	sip
lip	time
lime	ball
all	stood
crashes	jam

5. Write down the words that sound just like the thing it describes.
The first one is done for you.

a. Whoosh! went the wind.

b. Rip! went my pants.

c. When I ride my black mare she goes clippety-clop.

d. Pop! went the popcorn.

e. slippery, slithery snail.

Whoosh, _____

_____

MORE ACTION

• Read some of your favourite poems. Find the words that rhyme,
the beginning sounds that are repeated and the words that sound
like the thing itself. Make a list of them.

Poetry uses special effects
to work its magic. One is figurative language,
such as beginning sound repetition and rhyme. You will find poems
in your class library, the school library and the public library in your district.

Text Type:

FACTUAL RECOUNT

CAPITALS, COMMAS AND STOPS

Capital letters are needed to start sentences and proper nouns, such as people's names, special places and times, as in *Tillie, Taronga Park Zoo* and *Sunday*. The pronoun *I* always has a capital, as do the main words in headings, such as *At the Zoo*. **Commas** keep words apart in a list, as in *Tillie, Jock, Maria* ... **Full stops** come at the ends of sentences that are statements or commands. **Question marks** follow questions and **exclamation marks** follow exclamations. (See Units 15 and 16.)

At the Zoo

Last Sunday we went to Taronga Park Zoo. Tillie, Jock, Maria and Zara went with us. Do you know what we saw? There were lions, tigers, bears, seals and all sorts of birds, reptiles and fish. I liked the giraffes best. Wow! They are tall. What is your favourite animal, anyway?

1. *At the Zoo* shows you examples of capitals, commas, question marks and exclamation marks as they should be used in sentences. Punctuate the following.

a. nick   rob   yan   pedro   and   sarah   went   to   the   beach

b. have   you   seen   john

c. look   out

d. go   to   see   mrs   tiler

e. i   always   go   with   jan   jake   and   mary

2. Put commas and full stops in the correct places.

a. I saw giraffes lions tigers bears and seals

b. Echidnas kangaroos wombats and wallabies were at the zoo

c. We had sandwiches fruit ice cream and a drink for lunch

d. You will need to take a sweater a sun hat some sunscreen and some money

e. We went on the train the bus and on the ferry

3. Write full stops, question marks or exclamation marks at the ends of these sentences.

a. Look out

b. Where's your hat

c. Sit still and be quiet, please

d. I would like a pie for lunch

e. What a big gorilla

f. Have you seen Jake

g. I really like giraffes

h. Stop

MORE ACTION

• Write these again in your own book. Put in capital letters.

east hills school

rosie grant

france

japan

elm street

johnny potts

australia

new guinea

monday

mrs bowsprit

A factual recount tells about
something that happened in the past,
usually in order, one after another. You will find factual recounts
in books about the past, on television, in films and in much of the writing you do yourself.

Text Type:

NARRATIVE

SPEECH MARKS " "

Speech marks, or quotation marks as they are often called, are used around the actual words that someone says, as in
"Aha!" said the fire chief.

or

"I'm ready," Thomas said …
These words are called **direct speech.**

Thomas Torrington and the Fabulous Fire Suit

*"It's Mrs McNally," spluttered Thomas.
"She's locked herself out and left her keys inside and the kettle's on and …"*

"Aha!" said the Fire Chief. "This calls for action, immediate action." And he blew his whistle loudly. Beeeeeeeeep!

Thomas comes to the rescue, saves Mrs McNally and is given the fire suit he always wanted. In this story there are many examples of direct speech.

1. Finish these sentences from the story.

a. "_____," spluttered Thomas.

b. "_____!" said the Fire Chief.

(Note that commas, full stops, question marks and exclamation marks are inside the speech marks

2. Here are some more examples of direct speech from other parts of the stor
Add the quotation marks.

a. I'm short-staffed today, Thomas, said the friendly Fire Chief.

b. I'm ready, said Thomas. I'm ready to go.

c. Fine boy, that son of yours, said the Fire Chief. I'd like to make him a present of that fire suit for Christmas. Do you think he would like it?

d. I'm sure he would, said Thomas's mother.

e. Would I ever! said Thomas.

f. Happy Christmas, Thomas! said everyone.

3. Imagine it is Christmas. Finish the direct speech in the spaces in these sentences.

a. "I would like _____," I said to my mother and father.

b. "What would you like _____?" I asked my friends.

c. "Look what _____ for Christmas," I said to my friend, Sarah.

d. "Thank you for _____," I said to my grandmother.

e. "That's just what _____," I said to Mum and Dad.

4. Put the speech marks in the correct places in this paragraph.

Thomas Torrington was brave, I said to my teacher. He climbed the ladder by himself and opened the door. Do you think he deserved the present? my teacher asked. I sure do! I said. I would have been too scared. Wouldn't you?

MORE ACTION

- Write what you think happened in the story *Thomas Torrington and the Fabulous Fire Suit.*
- Write a conversation between Thomas and the Fire Chief before Thomas climbed the ladder. (The Fire Chief was too fat to get through the window of Mrs McNally's flat.)

A narrative tells a story. It contains things that happen to the characters and often has a surprise ending. You will read, see and hear narratives in books, at the movies, on the radio and on television.

TAKE A TEST 4

REVISION: UNITS 23-28

1. Cross out the wrong words.

a. My friend and (me, I) went swimming.

b. We (saw, seen) a shark.

c. The ship (sunk, sank).

d. He has (rang, rung) his mother.

e. (Wear, We're) going to a movie.

f. They (did, done) their best.

2. Fill in the correct word. Pick from the box.

> rang, rung;   sank, sunk;   did, done;   did, done;
> sang, sung;   sang, sung.

a. We _____ our friends on my mobile phone.

b. The old ship has _____ in deep water.

c. We _____ our homework.

d. We have _____ well in the test.

e. He _____ in the choir.

f. She has _____ in the choir.

3. Break these compound words into their parts. Write down the parts.
The first one is done for you.

classroom, eggshell, bookshelf, keyboard, pegboard, cupboard

class, room, _____

_____

4. Cross out the wrong homonym.

a. (Sum, Some) of my friends (where, wear) their uniforms to the shops.

b. I have (too, to, two) uniforms.

c. We have (bean, been) to school today.

d. Mum (knows, nose) best.

e. I let her (chews, choose) my size.

5. Cross out the wrong homonyms.

a. _(Their, There)_ are _(eight, ate)_ plants in _(our, hour)_ class garden.

b. She _(weighs, ways)_ _(for, four)_ kilograms more than I.

c. _(Hear, Here)_ are the boats on the _(blue, blew)_ _(see, sea)_ .

6. Draw boxes around the words that rhyme with *chip* in this poem.

Bits of Me

I can slap
with my hand.
I can pat
I can tip.
I can hop
with my leg.
I can run,
I can skip.

But what
can I do
with my chin
or my hip?
At least
with my lip
I can sip.   Gordon Winch

7. Write these sentences again. Put in the correct punctuation marks and capital letters.

a. where are my pyjamas b. I saw lions tigers bears and elephants c. look out

a. _____

b. _____

c. _____

8. Put in the speech marks.

a. Give me two, please, said Mandy.

b. Have you seen my dog? asked Charlie.

NONE WRONG (excellent)		1-2 WRONG (good)		3-4 WRONG (pass)		5 OR MORE WRONG (more work needed)	

Outcomes and Indicators

Key Outcomes Relating to Grammar

Although all English syllabus outcomes relate directly and indirectly to grammar, the following Talking and Listening, Reading and Writing outcomes provide the most tangible links with specific indicators in grammar understanding and learning.

New South Wales outcomes are used in this series – Teachers in other States should refer to specific State outcomes.

OUTCOMES CHECKLIST	Yes	Partly	No

Talking and Listening Outcomes

		Yes	Partly	No
TS1.1	Communicates with an increasing range of people for a variety of purposes on both familiar and introduced topics in spontaneous and structured classroom activities.	☐	☐	☐
TS1.2	Interacts in more extended ways with less teacher intervention, makes increasingly confident oral presentations and generally listens attentively.	☐	☐	☐
TS1.3	Recognises a range of purposes and audiences for spoken language and considers how own talking and listening are adjusted to different situations.	☐	☐	☐
TS1.4	Recognises that different types of predictable spoken texts have different organisational patterns and features.	☐	☐	☐

Reading Outcomes

		Yes	Partly	No
RS1.5	Reads a wider range of texts on less familiar topics with increasing independence and understanding, making connections between own knowledge and experience and information in texts.	☐	☐	☐
RS1.6	Draws on an increasing range of skills and strategies when reading and comprehending texts.	☐	☐	☐
RS1.7	Understands that texts are constructed by people and identifies ways in which texts differ according to their purpose, audience and subject matter.	☐	☐	☐
RS1.8	(Learning About Reading) Identifies the text structure and basic grammatical features of a limited range of text types.	☐	☐	☐

Writing Outcomes

WS1.9   Plans, reviews and produces a small range of simple literary and factual texts for a variety of purposes on familiar topics for known readers.   ☐ ☐ ☐

WS1.10   Produces texts using the basic grammatical features and punctuation conventions of the text type.   ☐ ☐ ☐

WS1.13   Identifies how own texts differ according to their purpose, audience and subject matter.   ☐ ☐ ☐

WS1.14   Identities the structure of own literary and factual texts and names a limited range of related grammatical features and conventions of written language.   ☐ ☐ ☐

INDICTORS CHECKLIST

1. Identifies and uses common nouns. (Unit 1)	☐	☐	☐
2. Identifies and uses proper nouns. (Unit 2)	☐	☐	☐
3. Identifies and uses descriptive adjectives. (Unit 3)	☐	☐	☐
4. Identifies and uses numeral adjectives. (Unit 4)	☐	☐	☐
5. Identifies and uses personal pronouns. (Unit 5)	☐	☐	☐
6. Identifies and uses possessive pronouns. (Unit 6)	☐	☐	☐
7. Identifies and uses action verbs. (Unit 7)	☐	☐	☐
8. Identifies and uses saying, thinking and feeling verbs. (Unit 8)	☐	☐	☐
9. Identifies and uses adverbs. (Unit 9)	☐	☐	☐
10. Identifies and uses prepositions. (Unit 10)	☐	☐	☐
11. Identifies and uses conjunctions. (Unit 11)	☐	☐	☐
12. Identifies and uses articles. (Unit 12)	☐	☐	☐
13. Recognises and uses noun groups. (Unit 13)	☐	☐	☐
14. Recognises and uses adverbial phrases. (Unit 14)	☐	☐	☐
15. Identifies and uses sentences. (Unit 15)	☐	☐	☐
16. Identifies and uses exclamations. (Unit 16)	☐	☐	☐
17. Identifies and uses commands. (Unit 17)	☐	☐	☐
18. Understands, identifies and uses clauses. (Unit 18)	☐	☐	☐
19. Identifies and uses compound sentences. (Unit 19)	☐	☐	☐
20. Understands and uses word links (cohesion) repetition and reference ties. (Unit 20)	☐	☐	☐
21. Identifies and uses synonyms and antonyms. (Unit 21)	☐	☐	☐
22. Identifies and uses connectives. (Unit 22)	☐	☐	☐
23. Understands and uses correct agreement and usage. (Unit 23)	☐	☐	☐
24. Recognises and uses compound words. (Unit 24)	☐	☐	☐
25. Understands and uses homonyms. (Unit 25)	☐	☐	☐
26. Identifies and uses repeated starting sounds and rhymes. (Unit 26)	☐	☐	☐
27. Understands and uses correct capitals, commas and stops. (Unit 27)	☐	☐	☐
28. Understands and uses speech marks. (Unit 28)	☐	☐	☐

Answers

UNIT 1

1. Beach, beach, bus, boys, girls, sand, parents, friends, boats, surfers, sea, rocks, waves, shop, apple, drink. **3.** towel, bucket, fish, sandcastle, spade. **4.** water, flag, sandwich, hat, bus, seaweed, dog, pool.

UNIT 2

1. Mick, Jess, Sally. **2., 3.** student's answers **4.** student's answers **5.** Algy, Algy, Algy; Emily Rose, Jack, Emily; Mary, Beecham's Pills; Mrs P., Mrs A., Mrs RRA., Mrs M., Mrs A., Mrs TTA., Parramatta.

UNIT 3

1. proud, grey, white, silver, dark, grey, brown **2.** grey rings, grey bill, grey legs, grey feet, young silver gull. **3.** a. silver, red, red, red, red.

UNIT 4

1. One, Two, Three, Four, Five, Six, Seven, Eight, Nine, Ten. **2.** juicy, tiny, yummy, lazy, rapid, shining, tasty, soaring, black, noisy. **3.** a. first, second. b. third. c. fourth, fifth. d. sixth. e. first. **4.** a. third, fourth, fifth. b. seven, nine. c. six, four, two. **5.** Across: 2. fifth. 3. three. 4. fourth. Down: 1. third. 2. five. 3. two.

UNIT 5

1. They, It, They, He, She. **2.** a. He, him. b. She, her. **3.** We, They, them, us, You, them. **4.** correct personal pronouns: a. them. b. We. c. I. d. You. e. I. **5.** a. He. He. b. It. c. They.

UNIT 6

1. mine, yours, mine, mine, yours, yours, theirs, his, hers, theirs. **2.** a. hers, his, yours, theirs, mine or ours. b. mine, hers, yours, theirs, or ours. c. theirs. **3.** a. yours. b. hers. c. theirs. d. yours. e. theirs. **4.** there are nine: hers, theirs, ours, his, mine, yours, hers, his, its.

UNIT 7

1. Get, Take, Cross, Run, Buy, Catch, Sit, Read, Leave. **2.** a. Step. b. Wait. c. Climb. d. Open. e. Move. **3.** student's answers. **4.** Ride, Walk, Row, Fly, Catch.

UNIT 8

1. a. wondered. b. knew. c. yelled. d. loved. e. think. **2.** saying: whisper, chatter, tell. thinking: think, wonder, know. feeling: dislike, hate, adore. **3.** a. whispered. b. thought. c. love. d. shouted. e. recited. **4.** student's answers.

UNIT 9

1. heavily, wildly, really, slowly, loudly, quickly, quietly, carefully. **2.** a. safely. b. softly. c. quickly. d. slowly. d. carefully. **3.** a. yesterday, today, tomorrow. b. later, now. c. soon. d. early. e. always. **4.** a. over. b. here. c. there. d. nearby. e. down. f. alongside. g. underneath. h. up. i. inside. j. outside. **5.** student's answers.

TAKE A TEST 1. REVISION: UNITS 1 – 9

1. common nouns: a. beach, bus, boats. b. birds, surfers, dogs. proper nouns: a. Jenny Smith. b. Cam, Bondi. c. Mrs O'Toole, Chan, Jason, Kakadu. **2.** descriptive adjectives a. tasty, soaring. b. fat, salty. c. tiny, toy. numeral adjectives: a. seven, eight. b. five. c. ten, ten, two. **3.** a. She. b. He. c. them. d. They. e. I. **4.** a. yours, mine, hers. b. his, theirs. **5.** a. run, jump, paddle, swim. b. Run, run, win. c. Read, eat. **6.** a. whispered. b. shouted. c. chatter, said. **7.** a. heavily, wildly. b. quickly, yesterday, early. **8.** a. quickly. b. loudly. c. softly. **9.** verbs: a. played. b. planted. adverbs: a. beautifully. b. carefully.

UNIT 10

1. a. from. b. with. c. on. d. from. e. with. f. in. g. to. h. for. i. in. j. into. **2.** possible answers: a. into or in. b. with. c. on. d. on. e. in. **3.** student's answers. **4.** in a boat. under a tree. over a fence. on a horse. with my mum, aunt, sister or nanny.

UNIT 11

2. a. and. b. but. c. and. d. but. e. and. **3.** a. unless. b. because. c. Although. d. Unless. e. because. **4.** a. I am seven and Louisa is too. b. I tried but I didn't catch anything. c. We went home because the fish did not bite. d. I am keen to go again because it was fun. e. It is fun at the beach unless it is raining.

UNIT 12

1. an, a, the, a, The, the, the, the, The, the, An, a, a, an **2.** a. an, the. b. An, a. c. The, the, an. d. an, a. e. an, a, the, the. **3.** a or the juicy pineapple; the ripest apple; an or the orange drink; an or the apple pie; the biggest mango; a or the bunch of grapes; a or the peach pie; a or the navel orange. **4.** a. the, the, the. b. a, a, a.

UNIT 13

1. a. bottlenose. b. open. c. long. d. little. e. with tiny. **2.** Danny Dolphin, a bottlenose dolphin. **3.** a. a dolphin, a bottlenose dolphin, a friendly bottlenose dolphin, a big friendly bottlenose dolphin. b. a mouth, an open mouth, a big open mouth, a big wide open mouth. c. Danny's teeth, Danny's top teeth, Danny's tiny top teeth, Danny's twenty tiny top teeth. (Question 3: words can be in different order.)

UNIT 14

1. a. through. b. on. c. near. d. under. e. with. f. in. g. among. h. over. i. in. j. with. **2.** a. under or in. b. on or at. c. in. d. with. e. on. **3.** student's answers. **4.** across: 2. inside. 3. through. 5. after. down: 1. under. 3. to. 4. over.

TAKE A TEST 2. REVISION: UNITS 10 – 14

1. on, under, near, over, through. **2.** a. over. b. in. c. behind. **3.** a. joining. join. b. and, and, and, but, and. **4.** a. an, a, the. b. A, an. **5.** the, the or an, a. **6.** bottlenose dolphin, open mouth, long nose, little fish. **7.** a. A tiny fish, the hungry dolphin. b. Two dolphins, clever tricks. **8.** a. through the air. b. in trees. c. in spring. d. with their beaks. **9.** a. on. b. in. c. under.

UNIT 15

1. a. 9. b. 4. c. 5. **2.** a. honey. b. six. c. sting. d. hives. e. buzzing. **3.** a. I saw the bees in the hive. b. Have you been stung by a bee? c. Do you like eating honey? d. A bee is an insect. e. Bees visit flowers. f. Do bees buzz? **4.** a. Bees live in hives. b. Bees like to visit flowers. c. You can hear the bees buzzing. d. The trees are in the forest. e. Do bees have knees?
5. student's answers.

UNIT 16

1. Look out! It will bite you! Jump, Julie! Jump! Yeow! Wow! **2.** Hooray! We've won! Let's go! I don't want any, thanks. What a cold day! Where are you going? Yum, yum! We sat very still. Ouch! Where's my coat? **3.** a. WOW, IT'S COLD! b. HE'S WON! c. YUM YUM! d. BE CAREFUL!

UNIT 17

1. student's answers. **2.** student's answers or a. SWIM BETWEEN THE FLAGS. b. COME OUT OF THE SUN. c. PUT ON SOME SUNSCREEN. d. GET THAT HAT ON. A full stop or exclamation is correct for them all, depending on the emphasis of the command.

UNIT 18

1. a. is my. b. is a. c. is brown, black. d. Biffo. e. biffs other. f. growl at. g. like. h. likes.
2. Biffo is my friend. Do you know why we call him Biffo? I like my dog, Biffo. Dogs are good pets. My friend, Maria has two pets at her place. He has a black ear and a brown ear.
3. We call him Biffo because he biffs other dogs. He is a mixture because he has different coloured ears. Biffo fights other dogs who growl and bark at me. Dogs make good pets if we look after them. I feed Biffo when he is hungry. I take Biffo for a walk after he has had his dinner. **4.** student's answers.

UNIT 19

1. a. it is the best team in the whole district. b. we are good sports, too. c. we clap them if they play well. d. she tells us to be good losers as well. **2.** a. 5. b. 10. c. student's answers.
3. student's answers. **4.** student's answers.

UNIT 20

1. b. you, He, me. **2.** a. they, him. b. He, them. c. him, he, her. **3.** a. He, him, you. b. he, him.
4. Pop 6, the 7, popcorn 7.

UNIT 21

1. student's answers. **2.** good, bad. hot, cold. over, under. interesting, boring. slim, stout. tough, tender. light, dark. near, far. inside, outside. quick, slow. **3.** 5. joyful, carefree, merry, cheerful, jolly. **4.** student's answers.

UNIT 22

1. First, Then, Next, Now, Afterwards, Finally, Now. **2.** a. First of all. b. Next. c. Finally.
3. student's answers. **4.** To begin I get dressed. Next I have my breakfast and clean my teeth.
Then I pack my school bag and now I'm ready to go.

TAKE A TEST 3. REVISION: UNITS 15 – 22

1. statement: Bees like flowers. or I still like bees, though. question: Did you know that bees
can sting? exclamation: Look out! **2.** a. book? b. out! c. sandwiches. d. pencil. e. mother?
3. Put on your sunscreen. Put on your T-shirt, now. **4.** My dog Biffo is clever. I take him for a
walk. **5.** Our team wins and we play fairly. We train hard and eat good food. We think our
team is best and we are proud of it. **6.** a. He. b. they, him. c. him. **7.** a. vile, ghastly. b. quick,
speedy. c. love, adore. **8.** a. First. b. Then. c. Finally.

UNIT 23

1. correct words: My, saw, did, my, I, We're, you, You're, my. **2.** a. did. b. done. c. did.
d. done. e. did. **3.** a. saw. b. seen. c. seen. d. saw. e. seen. **4.** a. sing. b. sung. c. sung. d. sung.
e. sing. **5.** across: 1. did. 2. seen. 3. rang. down: 1. done. 2. sang.

UNIT 24

1., 2. classroom, class, room; eggshell, egg, shell; pegboard, peg, board; handwriting, hand,
writing; chalkboard, chalk, board; cupboards, cup, boards; bookshelves, book, shelves;
keyboards, key, boards; Raindrop, rain, drop; Hardcastle, hard, castle. **3.** playground,
goalkeeper, sunlight, playtime, outside. **4.** pineapple, strawberry, passionfruit, watermelon,
grapefruit, blackberry.

UNIT 25

1. correct words: Some, wear, not, too, dear, buy, not, wear, be, to, way, to, There, two, ways.
2. correct words: a. no. b. been. c. choose. d. knows. e. Our. **3.** student's answers.
4. their, sew, sow; been; poor; sea; blew; scent; eight; sure; for, fore; here; rode.

UNIT 26

1. a. S sounds: Simon's special singlet, stripes, Simon, singlet, Simon, slip, swim, special
singlet. b. white, night; swim, him. **2.** s, f, m, p, b. **3.** You've never met a mice before. right
to your toes. **4.** ham, jam; good, stood; lip, sip; lime, time; all, ball; crashes, smashes.
5. a. Whoosh b. Rip. c. clippety-clop. d. Pop. e. slippery, slithery.

UNIT 27

1. a. Nick, Rob, Yan, Pedro and Sarah went to the beach. b. Have you seen John? c. Look
out! d. Go to see Mrs Tiler. e. I always go with Jan, Jake and Mary. **2.** a. I saw giraffes, lions,
tigers, bears and seals. b. Echidnas, kangaroos, wombats and wallabies were at the zoo. c. We
had sandwiches, fruit, ice cream and a drink for lunch. d. You will need to take a sweater, a
sun hat, some sunscreen and some money. e. We went on the train, the bus and on the ferry.
3. a. Look out! b. Where's your hat? c. Sit still and be quiet, please. d. I would like a pie for
lunch. e. What a big gorilla! f. Have you seen Jake? g. I really like giraffes. h. Stop!

UNIT 28

1. a. "It's Mrs McNally," b. "Aha!" **2.** a. "I'm short-staffed today, Thomas," said the friendly Fire Chief. b. "I'm ready," said Thomas. "I'm ready to go." c. "Fine boy, that son of yours," said the Fire Chief. "I'd like to make him a present of that fire suit for Christmas. Do you think he would like it?" d. "I'm sure he would," said Thomas's mother. e. "Would I ever!" said Thomas. f. "Happy Christmas, Thomas!" said everyone. **3.** student's answers.
4. "Thomas Torrington was brave," I said to my teacher. "He climbed the ladder by himself and opened the door." "Do you think he deserved the present?" my teacher asked. "I sure do!" I said. "I would have been too scared. Wouldn't you?"

TAKE A TEST 4. REVISION: UNITS 23 – 28

1. correct words: a. I. b. saw. c. sank. d. rung. e. We're. f. did. **2.** a. rang. b. sunk. c. did. d. done. e. sang. f. sung. **3.** class, room; egg, shell; book, shelf; key, board; peg, board; cup, board. **4.** correct homonyms: a. Some, wear. b. two. c. been. d. knows. e. choose. **5.** correct homonyms: a. There, eight, our. b. weighs, four. c. Here, blue sea. **6.** tip, skip, hip, lip, sip.
7. a. Where are my pyjamas? b. I saw lions, tigers, bears and elephants. c. Look out!
8. a. "Give me two, please," said Mandy. b. "Have you seen my dog?" asked Charlie.